WRITE IT.
FORGET IT.
IF YOU CAN

Book Design by HMDpublishing

CONTENTS

Part VII.
Extras **192**

INTRODUCTION

Memory can be a fascinating, elusive, wholly frustrating thing.

Why is it we can perfectly remember the hazelnut latte and cranberry scone we had that one time at that little airport café on a layover in Boston (the coffee was slightly weak; your luggage had a broken wheel and caused you no end of aggravation), yet completely blank out when a medical form asks for our child's birth date?

Why does the smell of your grandmother's house jump to mind easily, yet its address has long since faded in the rearview?

Believe it or not, memory is not random, even if it seems that way. Everything your brain stores, it does so for a reason. And, likewise, everything it forgets is done for a specific purpose, as well.

There are three processes involved in memory: encoding, storage, and recall. Encoding is the input, or every piece of information your brain gets during a particular moment, from each of your five senses. Storage is where that memory goes: short-term, and long-term.

Recall is the process by which we retrieve those memories that make it through the gauntlet into long-term storage— and it's one of the trickiest things to do.

Fortunately, memory recall can be optimized and strengthened through practice. First, though, it helps to understand how recalling memories works.

EMOTIONS AND MEMORY RECALL

Psychologists and neuroscientists have studied memory as long as they've studied the brain itself. While there's no simple answer as to why we forget certain things and retain others, there is one clue: emotions.

Maya Angelou once said, "I've learned that people will forget what you said, people will forget what you did, but people will never forget how you made them feel."

Feelings: that's the shortest explanation for the seemingly erratic rules of memory recall.

When an event has strong feelings attached to it—for better, or for worse—the brain takes notice. It decides something about that moment must be important, or else we wouldn't be having such a strong reaction.

Think of it like the little star or flag icons on your email inbox: the mind puts a small Note to Self on that memory, and it becomes less likely it'll get chucked into the Recycling Bin.

Now, the brain may not be able to remember *why* that moment was so important—and goodness knows, we can't figure it out—but it does know, "This was emotional. It elicited a stronger than average response. It should probably stick around."

Furthermore, it's far easier to remember how something made us feel than the actual details.

Think about it: as many times as you may blank on your child's birthday (a fact you probably *do* know, as well or even better than your own birthday), you've likely never, ever forgotten how their actual birth made you feel.

You may not recall the hospital room, or the color of their nursery blanket.

Your doctor or nurse's name might escape you completely. The weather outside your window: a total mystery.

But without a doubt, you can recall with vivid clarity the exhaustion, relief, and unparalleled joy when the baby was placed into your arms.

Or your grandmother's house—can you remember the street it was on? Where the utensils were stored in the kitchen? How many bathrooms or television sets there were?

Probably not. But you *can* remember the scent of her house, or any beloved relative's home. You may not remember specific holidays or visits, but you remember the emotions behind them: the excitement as a child of running through the door; perhaps the solemnity of stricter rules than your own household, feeling like a weight from the moment you crossed the threshold; or the comfortable buzz of conversation from adults, while you played with your cousins or your grandmother's cat.

These are just examples, of course, but if you follow the same train of thought, it's likely you *can* recall a large amount of detail from any point in your life. They might not be the details you deem important—but, once upon a time, your brain did, thanks to the high emotions attached.

While emotional ties are a strong factor in memory recall, however, they're far from the be-all, end-all. In fact, there are several theories out there as to how memory functions.

THEORIES OF MEMORY

Smell itself is another factor. Because scents are processed directly in the olfactory bulb, which is connected to the amygdala and hippocampus, the mind likely stores smells in a totally different way from other sensory cues.[1]

Other theories state that repetition will help our brains flag certain pieces of information for retention, or that our minds function more like computers—processing visual and auditory cues separately. Some say the more we think about something, the more likely it is we'll remember it.[2]

There are also memory anomalies, such as false memories—remembering events differently than how they really happened, or things that did not happen at all. You've undoubtedly been at a dinner party or family holiday, sharing an anecdote you'd swear on your life happened...only for someone at the table to point out all the details you got wrong.

Influenced memories are another strange but fascinating occurrence. These are things we don't *actually* recall, but

1 https://www.discovery.com/science/Why-Smells-Trigger-Such-Vivid-Memories

have been told so many times our brains created visualizations to accompany the story.

Growing up, you were probably told about your own birth hundreds of times. Logically, you know you can't remember it...but you might have a mental snapshot or two of the events, nonetheless. This is because your brain, after hearing the details so many times, decided you needed a few visual cues to complete the story.

Interference happens frequently, too: an old memory interfering with the retention or processing of a new one, or vice-versa. Ever called a new dog by the old one's name, or driven to a friend's old address despite knowing they moved clear across town? That's the old information interfering with the new. It's also a reason habits can be so difficult to break: sometimes, we just plain forget what we're supposed to be doing.[3]

"Flash bulb" moments are another kind of memory. These events are sometimes traumatic—a brief feeling of terror before a car accident, or how badly your hands were shaking as you undid your seatbelt following the collision, for example.

Other times, though, the events don't have any personal connection: they were just so significant to the world around us, our brains formed clear, vivid logs of where we were when the event happened. The death of renowned figures, natural disasters, declarations of war, the moon landing—any moment where it felt like the earth stood still, in shock or in awe, can trigger a flash bulb memory.

---

3 Ibid.

WHY DOES UNDERSTANDING MEMORY MATTER?

This book opened with a bit of a crash course on memory for one simple reason: when you understand how memory functions, you can better recall details and events you think you've long forgotten.

Until you were asked to recall your child's birth, or the scent of that beloved relative's house...were you fully, consciously aware that you remembered those things?

Or, if you did know you remembered them—were you surprised at how vivid the memories still were?

Sometimes memories feel gone, but are really just dormant: buried in our subconscious, waiting for the right prompt. We might not think about these details every day, or even most days. We might go years without recalling some of them, in fact.

But when we consciously command those memories to the surface, we're able to focus on them, bring elements of them back into full-color, and even use them to remember more than we might have thought possible.

Try it again. Imagine that relative's home once more. Think of a sibling, or cousin, with whom you used to play during family dinners or holidays.

If you focus hard enough, you might be able to remember exactly how they looked—not in photographs or videos, and not as they are today, but exactly as they looked to you back then: the same low and close angle of a hidden fortress under the dining table; the spray of freckles across their nose; the stifled laughter you exchanged after doing something sneaky.

You can probably remember even more, too, like a strange old doll on a shelf that always scared you, or a pattern on the wallpaper you stared at while you were scolded.

All those new details might feel as though they've descended out of the blue, suddenly dawning on you—but you've remembered them all along. You just forgot that you remembered.

WHAT IS THIS BOOK FOR?

This will be far more than a catalog of bullet-pointed details. While some questions will be simple and straightforward (your parents' names, for example), others will ask you to dig deeper into your memory.

With this book, you'll leave not just an account of what your life was, but *how* it was.

Your children, grandchildren, and future descendants can read this book and feel what you felt, smell what you smelled, and vividly imagine how you lived. If that sounds egotistical, consider how much you would have loved a book like this, written by a beloved relative.

And it's not just for other people, nor meant to sit idly on a shelf until you're gone: this book will help you keep your own memory sharp, not only in writing it, but in rereading it throughout the years to come.

Research shows journaling helps mental health and that, while writing, our brains behave quite similarly to those of athletes, musicians, or anyone completing complex tasks.[4]

4 https://www.nytimes.com/2014/06/19/science/researching-the-brain-of-writers.html

Writing engages several areas of the brain at once—and writing about our own memories does even more.

Not only can reading in general help prevent or slow the progression of memory decline,[5] but specifically reading old journals, or a book like this one, can also improve memory, increase one's self-esteem, and provide a sense of fulfillment.[6]

Granted, the most research in this area—known as "reminiscence therapy"—has been targeted towards dementia patients, but that doesn't make it any less applicable to those without dementia, nor any less fascinating.

When you reflect back on your life thus far, you're able to focus not just on your regrets, worries for the future, or current trials, but on all you've experienced and accomplished: the good, the bad, the beautiful, the ugly...everything that's made you who you are now.

HOW TO USE THIS BOOK

The beauty of an autobiography is that it's not the exact, harsh, calculated truth. It's simply *your* truth.

It's okay if you come across a question you can't answer. Simply write "I don't remember," and move on.

Alternatively, you can write, "I'm not sure, but I think it happened this way...."

This is your autobiographical journal. There are no wrong answers. You're not setting out to write about your life exactly as it happened: you're writing about your life exactly as you experienced it. And that account will be far richer than a simple (and, frankly, quite dull) list of verifiable details.

To be fair, some details are important, but not nearly as much as we might think. What would you rather know about a dear loved one: the name of their elementary school, or how they met their best friend on the playground after engaging in a schoolyard fight?

In other words: don't sweat the small stuff.

If you're looking for a book to precisely catalog those minute details, this isn't it. Every section, from early childhood to one's golden years, is crafted to start at the surface—with those "easy" details—but then drill down, deeper and deeper, to what really matters.

HELPFUL HINTS TO RECALL MEMORIES

As you've read—and definitely experienced firsthand—memory is an odd process. There are some things we really *have* forgotten: events totally wiped from our minds that we desperately wish we could get back. These forgotten details are frustrating, and might make you wonder why the brain deemed them unimportant. Clearly, they weren't.

But for every truly forgotten memory, there are hundreds more merely...sleeping. This book is designed to wake them up.

With that in mind, here are some tips to more efficiently recall memory, and to help you get the most out of your autobiographical journal.

- **Carry this book with you everywhere, at least initially.** You might not recall certain details while writing, but the mere act of trying to remember can set your brain in motion to retrieve those details. They'll dawn on you when you least suspect it: while doing dishes, pumping gas, or even falling asleep. Keep this book nearby so you can dive back in when the memory is still fresh. Once you've completed it to (or close to) your current age, you can set it aside for a while.

- **Set a reminder to revisit this book regularly.** The week before your birthday is a good time to check this journal. You'll be able to read through everything you've written so far—increasing mental acuity, yes, but also enjoying some well-earned nostalgia after another trip around the sun—and take stock of your year so far, filling in new memories as desired.

- **Write in solitude.** They say writing is a lonely profession...and journaling should be, too. Our brains operate best when we can fully concentrate on the task at hand, free from distraction or conversation. Isolation will also help you to truly lose yourself in memories. It's a bit like falling asleep: there's a period of time, as you're falling into unconsciousness, when you can't be disturbed, or else the process has to start all over. Diving into your memory banks is the same way, so make sure interruptions are minimal or non-existent before you begin.

- **Write in the early mornings, if possible.** The reason for this is two-fold. Firstly, there will be days when working on your autobiographical journal feels like a chore. It might be when you reach the section on your teenage years (a time most of us would love to forget but, unfortunately, remember all too well), or just because you're so tired after work, writing is the last thing on your mind. It's easier to get your hardest tasks done first thing, so they don't haunt you the rest of the day. And secondly, your brain is usually the most alert in the mornings, even if it doesn't feel like it. By mid-afternoon, most of us get into a slump, and don't recover until dinnertime. If you wait to write until noon or later, you're not taking advantage of your clearest thinking window.

- **Meditate first, or simply rest.** It's easier to remember things when we're relaxed and calm. Take a few mo-

ments to sit or lie perfectly still, focus on nothing but
your breathing...and simply be. You'll then approach this
journal with clarity, calmness, and openness.

- **Don't tell anyone else about the book—yet.** Have you
ever noticed that buzzing excitement and fresh ambition
when you get a new idea? Maybe it's plans for a diet and
exercise program, a new business venture, or painting
that guest bathroom a color you've always wanted. But
then you shared your idea with someone else and, re-
gardless of their reaction...the excitement and ambition
diminished, or went away altogether. Research suggests
sharing our goals, especially publicly, makes us less likely
to accomplish them.[7] To keep the excitement bubble from
bursting, keep your journal to yourself for now. This increases the likelihood you'll consistently write in it. It's
okay if a few people, especially those who will eventual-
ly inherit the journal, know about it—but don't let them
read passages until it's up to date or finished.

- **When you get stuck, have a conversation...with yourself.** Our writing brain is different from our speech cen-
ters. You've probably noticed that, while your writing is
similar to the way you talk, it's far from identical—and
that it's easier to talk out loud than it is to write the same
idea on paper. When you get stuck on a section in your
journal, have a conversation with yourself: read what
you've written so far, then finish it out loud. New details
will come to mind easily, and you'll be able to go back and
fill in what you missed.

- **Lose yourself in imagination.** If you can't remember
your favorite elementary school teacher, can you remember the bus ride? The classroom? How scary it was get-

---

7 https://blog.trello.com/science-backed-reasons-you-shouldnt-share-
your-goals#:~:text=In%202009%2C%20Gollwitzer%20and%20
his,the%20work%20to%20achieve%20it.&text=Researchers%20
concluded%20that%20when%20someone,you%20to%20reduce%20
your%20efforts.

ting called to write on the blackboard? Close your eyes and immerse yourself in the pieces you *do* remember. The rest might follow—and if it doesn't, that's okay. Just capture the pieces you do recall.

- **Trigger memories with objects.** School supplies, favorite outfits in storage, and photographs can trigger memories because the brain says, "Hey, we've seen this thing before!" You can then choose to write about the item itself, or wait and see if it sparks any new memories.

- **Practice serial recall.** If you're having trouble remembering your family's old holiday traditions, start at the beginning. What were Christmas mornings like? Were you and your siblings allowed to storm the pile of presents as soon as you awoke, or were you required to wait patiently for your parents to wake up, too? Starting with one simpler detail can help you "trace the chain" until you reach those links you've forgotten.

- **Give yourself permission to be wrong.** One of the hardest things about writing is our tendency to self-edit as we go. This disrupts our thought processes, our "flow state" (the ability to completely lose ourselves in the task at hand), and slows progress *way* down. Ignore misspellings, messy handwriting, and even factual errors until the very end of your writing session for that day. And don't judge yourself: if you think you're misremembering something, or can't remember it at all, say so. It happens to all of us.

One more note before you begin....

Parts I through VI are presented in chronological order: Childhood, Teen Years, Early Adulthood, Twenties and Thirties, Forties and Fifties, and Sixties and Beyond. Part VII, however, is entitled "Extras," and can be filled out at any age, or across multiple years.

It's recommended you skim it now, or as soon as you finish your most current section. You'll then know what each entry entails, and have a good idea of when you'd like to tackle it.

Introduction

PART I:
YOUR CHILDHOOD

Childhood memories haven't gotten much spotlight in the way of scientific research until fairly recently. For a long time, it was believed that kids just didn't have good memory processes.[8]

Today, we know that's definitely not the case. Children have remarkable memory, and can recall details that adults miss entirely.

One reason for this is, as mentioned earlier, the emotions attached to those memories. Children feel things very strongly: when they're happy, sad, energetic, or scared, the emotion tends to consume them at its peak. Most children don't just feel happiness; they feel absolute joy. When they're sad, even over something seemingly minor, they can often feel devastated.

Frustrating as this is as a parent (why does one simple "no, you can't have that candy" cause full-blown tantrums?), it's immensely helpful to us now! Our ability to recall our earliest memories is heightened because of those emotional ties.

As you complete this section, try to focus on the emotional aspects as much as the details. Not only will the details come to you more easily, but you'll also find your descriptions of your childhood turn out richer and fuller.

8 https://www.theatlantic.com/health/archive/2015/07/why-childhood-memories-disappear/397502/

MY BEGINNINGS

I was born on ....

in...

This is the story of my birth, as told to me by ....

....

....

....

....

....

....

....

....

....

....

....

My full birth name was ....

....

I was named after the following people, or because of these

reasons: ....

....

....

....

....

....

....

....

....

....

....

....

....

....

....

....

....

....

I always [liked/disliked] my name because.....................................

....

....

....

....

....

I feel my name [suits/doesn't suit me] because ....

....

....

....

....

....

If I had to rename myself, I'd go with ....

due to...

....

....

....

....

....

....

....

My earliest memory is...

....

....

....

....

....

....

....

....

....

....

I was about this old: ....

The emotions I felt during that time were...

....

....

....

....

I think this memory stuck with me because.....................................

....

....

....

....

....

....

....

....

....

....

What I looked like as a child: ....

-Hair color and texture...

....

....

-My hairstyle was usually...

....

....

-I liked/didn't like my hair because...

....

....

....

....

....

....

....

-My eye color was...

-My height was: (average, shorter than average, taller than average) ....

....

....

....

....

....

....

....

....

....

I think I was like this as a child: ....

....

....

....

....

....

....

Other people often described me as...

....

....

....

....

....

....

....

....

....

....

These descriptions were (accurate/inaccurate/partially accurate) because..

....

....

....

....

....

....

....

....

....

....

....

....

....

....

....

....

MY CHILDHOOD HOME

Our childhood home is the stage upon which our entire young world was first set.

Our days began and ended there. Balmy summer nights were spent in the backyard. Cold and rainy days passed listening to the storm against the roof. We played hide-and-seek in the nooks and crannies we still remember to this day.

If the brain does indeed function like a computer, then our childhood home is worthy of its own hard drive: it's the backdrop of most of our childhood memories, and you can likely still remember every detail with barely any effort.

Before starting this next section, take a moment to close your eyes, breathe, and picture that home again. Put yourself back in your old bedroom, or your favorite seat at the dinner table.

For just a few minutes, be a kid again.

The home where I grew up was located in: ....

....

....

It was this style of a house/apartment/etc.: ....

....

....

....

....

....

Its decor would now be described as ....

but as a child, I thought it was...

....

....

....

Overall, I remember my home smelling like: ....

....

....

....

....

....

My favorite hiding spot in the house was..

....

....

....

A unique detail I remember about the house is.............................

....

....

....

An aspect of my home that others would find small or incon-

sequential, but that I still remember well, is its.............................

....

....

Something I used to hate about that house, but now miss,

would be...

....

....

....

....

....

....

....

If I had to describe the floors, I'd use these words: ....

....

....

....

....

An activity I wasn't allowed to do in the house was ....

....

....

....

....

....

I [obeyed the rules/did it anyway]..

....

....

....

These are the directions to my old bedroom, from the front

door: ....

....

....

....

....

....

....

My bedroom was: [Circle all that apply] (small, cozy, big, open, cramped, comfortable, almost always messy, usually clean, organized, chaotic, colorful, muted, bright, dark, shared, all mine, decorated how I wanted, decorated to my parents' tastes, coordinated, filled with mismatched furniture, my place of refuge, a place I associated with being punished, my playroom, for sleeping only, quiet, loud, peaceful, wild) ....

....

....

Some personal touches I added to my room include................

....

....

....

....

....

....

....

....

....

....

Posters, photos, or other decor I kept on my walls:......................

....

....

....

....

....

....

....

....

....

....

....

....

....

....

I remember this most vividly about my bedroom: ....

....

....

....

....

....

....

....

....

....

....

....

....

....

....

I enjoyed keeping my door (open/closed) because.....................

....

....

....

Something from my childhood bedroom I still own is ....

....

....

....

I kept it all these years because..

....

....

....

....

....

My parents' bedroom was [open to me/off-limits], and I re-member these details about how it looked, smelled, and felt:

....

....

....

....

....

....

....

....

A favorite detail from my siblings' bedrooms is..........................

....

....

....

....

....

My favorite room in the entire house was ....

because of its..

....

....

....

When I was ...., I broke this item in our home: ....

....

....

....

....

I got [away with it/in trouble]. Here's what I remember about

how it happened ....

....

....

....

....

....

....

....

....

....

....

....

If I could have one piece of furniture from my childhood home in my current home, it would be ...., because..

....

....

....

Outside, our yard was [big, small, non-existent]. One of my earliest memories of the space outside my home is............................

....

....

....

....

....

....

....

....

....

On rainy or cold days in our home, you'd find me.............................

....

....

....

....

....

Other homes I lived in as a child, or houses where I spent a great deal of time, include: ....

....

....

....

....

....

....

My Childhood Home

Some details I remember very well about those places are....

....

....

....

....

....

....

....

....

....

....

....

....

....

....

....

....

....

....

MY FAMILY

Just like our childhood homes were the first places we explored, memorized, and treasured, our families were probably the first people we met, interacted with, and loved. They shaped our personalities. Most likely, they were the cause of our first laughs...as well as our first fights.

In them, we learned happiness, frustration, coexistence (impossible as that may have felt, sometimes), and what it meant to trust others implicitly.

In this section, you'll document your parents and siblings, your impressions and memories of them, and how they shaped your life, both as you grew up and today.

Don't feel limited to your nuclear family if other people had an equal or more prominent role in your daily life, though. If you grew up in a multi-generational household, had stepparents or stepsiblings, or lived with non-family members, feel free to modify these questions as you see fit.

The same holds true if the terms "mother" and "father" don't fit with your particular situation (example: if you were raised by grandparents, aunts or uncles, or same-sex parents). If you were an only child, you can choose to skip the Siblings section, or fill it out with memories of people who *felt* like siblings: close cousins, neighborhood kids, or childhood best friends.

Finally, remember the definition of truth we covered earlier: this book isn't about 100% factual accuracy. Instead, it's meant to be an accurate log of your memories—the way you perceived your family.

If you get stuck, take a break and get creative: look at old family photos, watch a movie you and your siblings loved as kids, or call one of them up and chat a while. You can even try asking what they remember, to see if their recollections spark any of your own.

MY PARENTS

My parents' names were: ....

....

....

My mother's job was: ....

....

My father's job was: ....

....

In a word, my father's temperament was ....

while my mother's was ....

.... Overall, I think they [clashed/complemented each

other] because ....

....

....

....

I was closest to my [mother/father] for these reasons: ....

....

....

....

....

....

....

....

....

....

....

....

Adjectives that describe my father best: [Circle all that apply] (Animated, mellow, extroverted, introverted, bold, soft-spoken, organized, scattered, distant, involved, hot-tempered, laid-back, funny, serious, optimistic, pessimistic, spontaneous, inhibited, high-energy, calm) ....

....

....

Adjectives that describe my mother best: [Circle all that apply] (Animated, mellow, extroverted, introverted, bold, soft-spoken, organized, scattered, distant, involved, hot-tempered, laid-back, funny, serious, optimistic, pessimistic, spontaneous, inhibited, high-energy, calm) ....

....

....

Traits I inherited from my parents, and where I got each one, include: ....

....

....

....

....

....

....

....

....

....

....

....

....

....

....

....

The greatest thing my father taught me was..................................

....

....

The greatest thing my mother taught me was..............................

....

....

What my parents and I fought about most often while I was

growing up was..

....

....

....

....

....

....

....

....

....

....

Something I wish my parents had done differently is.....................

....

....

....

....

....

....

Something I think they did very well raising me is.....................

....

....

....

....

....

....

One thing I will/did do differently when raising my own kids

is ....

....

....

for the following reasons: ....

....

....

....

....

....

....

The worst punishment my parents ever gave me was ....

.... and

I got it because ....

....

....

....

....

....

....

....

....

As an adult, I think they [were very fair/overreacted]................

....

....

A happy memory of my parents that sticks with me to this

day is..

....

....

....

....

....

It's special to me because ....

....

....

....

....

....

....

My father's hobbies and interests included.................................

....

....

....

....

My mother's hobbies and interests included ....

....

....

....

....

Some special items that my parents owned which always fas-

cinated me were...

....

....

....

....

....

....

....

When I was sick or upset, I could always count on my [moth-

er/father] to ....

....

....

....

....

....

....

....

....

....

My [mother/father] taught me most of what I use in my daily life as an adult..

....

....

I felt [understood/misunderstood] by my father ....

....

....

I felt [understood/misunderstood] by my mother ....

....

....

....

....

....

My parents never failed to...

....

....

....

....

....

Something about my parents I took for granted as a kid, but

really appreciate now, is...

....

....

....

....

....

....

....

....

....

....

....

....

MY SIBLINGS

Our brothers and sisters are our first peer group: the kids we grew up with, the young adults we matured with, and the only people on this earth whose life experiences come incredibly close to matching our own. They were our first allies, or our first bullies (or, more often, both).

There's no need to sugarcoat your responses anywhere in this journal, but especially here: sibling relationships are complicated, even in adulthood. It's common to feel varying or mixed feelings about our brothers and sisters, from an enduring closeness to endless frustration,[9] yet still love them even when times are tough, or the relationship becomes strained.

Again, if you don't have siblings (or are no longer close to them), you can decide to skip this section, or use it for close cousins or friends, instead.

---

9 https://www.psychologies.co.uk/importance-siblings

In total, I have/had this many siblings: ....

Names	how many years older or younger they are

....

....

....

....

Growing up, ...

was the funniest kid in our family. A great story about them I

still love today is...

....

....

....

....

....

....

....

....

....

....

....

....

....

The sibling that annoyed me most was ....,

because..

....

....

My favorite sibling to play with was ....,

because of how they ....

....

....

....

....

....

....

A lesson each sibling taught me, even if they didn't know it,

is...

....

....

....

....

....

....

....

....

....

....

....

....

Something silly we used to do/enjoy is.......................................

....

....

....

....

....

....

A cherished childhood memory I still have with each sibling

is..

....

....

....

....

....

....

....

....

....

....

....

....

....

The traits I admire most in each sibling are: ....

....

....

....

....

....

....

....

Ways in which we're wildly different include...............................

....

....

....

....

....

....

....

....

A memory with my siblings I'm still mad about is.........................

....

....

....

....

....

....

....

....

....

A secret my siblings and I have kept from our parents to this day, or for many years afterwards, is: ....

....

....

....

....

....

My connection with my siblings has shaped my adult life in these ways: ....

....

....

....

....

....

....

....

....

....

....

....

....

....

....

....

....

....

....

....

....

....

....

MY GRANDPARENTS

If you were fortunate enough to know your grandparents, you were given a unique blessing: your grandmothers and grandfathers likely held the same unconditional love for you as your parents, but with the wisdom of hindsight to soften its edges. After all, that's a big benefit of having kids: to one day enjoy your grandkids, without all the frustration and headaches of raising them!

Grandparents are a living link to our family's roots and history. They provided support and encouragement our own parents sometimes couldn't, helped care for us, and raised the people who raised us. Even if you weren't close to yours, or didn't get much time with them, fill out this section to the best of your ability. Any insight on your grandparents is, in the end, a little more insight on yourself, too.

My grandparents' names were...

....

....

....

....

Their occupations were..

....

....

....

....

....

....

They grew up during..

....

....

....

....

....

....

....

....

....

....

....

....

Overall, each grandparent's personality was...............................

....

....

....

....

....

....

....

The grandparent I was closest to was ....

I think I was closer to them than the others because.................

....

....

....

....

....

....

A story my grandfather/grandmother told me about their

own childhood is...

....

....

....

....

....

....

....

....

....

....

....

....

A cherished memory I have of each grandparent is......................

....

....

....

....

....

....

....

....

....

....

....

....

Something I always admired about my grandparents was: ......

....

....

....

....

....

....

....

MY PETS

There's something incredible about connecting with a family member who's not even the same species as you. Our childhood pets were likely our first real link to the natural world; many of them taught us responsibility and compassion long before we knew what those words meant.

Some may be fortunate enough to still have their childhood pets around, but most of us said goodbye to those furry friends long ago. While this section might be difficult, consider it a kind of catharsis: an opportunity to recall your pet's life in vivid color, and not to dwell on their passing.

That said, of course, this is your journal—so feel free to use the blank lines at the end of this section to detail the loss of your pet, if you wish.

Recalling painful or sad memories is often easier than remembering happy ones.[10] This is theorized to happen because our brains often hone in on specific details, assuming we need to process whatever's causing those unpleasant emotions. For example, you might remember the symptoms of a beloved pet's illness, or the vet's office where you said goodbye, but have trouble recalling exact instances where you and your pet played together.

---

10 Source: https://www.livescience.com/1827-bad-memories-stick-good.html

Rest assured, this is normal—and it's okay if your answers in this section are limited or vague, as a result.

Likewise, it's perfectly fine if you choose to skip this section because you can't remember your childhood pets very well, or had little to no connection with them. Alternatively, you can choose to write about an animal you remember very well from your childhood, but that may not have belonged to you, such as your aunt's cat or a neighbor's dog.

Lastly, if you had multiple pets you want to reminisce about, you can use the extra lines provided at the end of this section to do so.

My childhood pet's name was ....,

a [female/male] [animal type]..

....

My family got our pet [before I was born/when I was ....

years old]. The way we acquired our pet was.................................

....

....

....

....

His/her coloring was ....

My pet slept in ....,

and spent most of its day ....

....

....

My pet's personality was [energetic, calm, happy, reserved,

loving, aloof, playful, serious].

....

....

....

....

....

My pet's favorite activity was ....

....

....

....

Something I loved doing with my pet was.......................................

....

....

....

....

Some tricks my pet could perform, or some interesting quirks

they had were..

....

....

....

....

Fun memories I have of my pet include...

....

....

....

....

I think my first memory of my pet is...

....

....

....

....

A funny story about that pet I still remember is...........................

....

....

....

....

....

....

....

What I miss most about my childhood pet is.................................

....

....

....

....

....

....

My Pets

MY CHILDHOOD HOBBIES AND INTERESTS

Interestingly, this might be the section of your autobiographical journal that changes your entire life for the better: psychologists believe that revisiting childhood hobbies and interests makes us happier.[11]

Part of it's the nostalgia factor, like how happy memories in general can improve neurological functions and mood—but there's something deeper to it, as well.

When we were kids, almost everything interested us. Everything seemed possible. We picked up instruments without a single thought of technical precision or the thousands of practice hours that lay ahead; we could only picture ourselves as famous rock or pop stars. When we painted pictures, we did so without the burdensome refrains of "art isn't

11 *https://thriveglobal.com/stories/meghan-markle-theater-visit-acting-happiness-hobby/*

a real job" that judgemental (and wrong) adults would later put into our heads.

In other words, we immersed ourselves completely into the activities we loved.

Then adulthood crept in.

Suddenly, we had majors to choose in college, and practical jobs to look for, and medical benefits to worry about. Odds and probabilities rang in our heads, whenever we thought about our old dreams of becoming musicians, ballerinas, world leaders, or astronauts. Life got real, and it got hard. We had families to feed, mortgages to pay, and endless chores to complete.

While the loss of some favorite hobbies and interests is inevitable (trust us, it's not the end of the world if you no longer enjoy making mud pies), there's a good chance we lost a big piece of ourselves—and our happiness—every time another one fell away, replaced by something more "adult."

As you complete this section, really dig into why you loved those hobbies. True, you may no longer care about becoming a rock star—but you might find you miss your old guitar way more than you thought. Your days of biking through the woods until the streetlights beckoned you home can turn into weekly rides with your kids or spouse, recapturing a little bit of the rush you remember from your youth.

And, before you discount a return to childhood hobbies as...well, childish, consider this: research shows engaging in nostalgic activities makes you feel less lonely, more valued, and rejuvenated.[12]

Besides—when you consider how energetic and optimistic you were as a kid, and how much brighter the world seemed... is being "childish" really so bad?

---

12 https://ifstudies.org/blog/nostalgia-reveals-the-importance-of-family-and-close-relationships

My favorite show as a kid was ....

....

....

....

....

I still remember this episode....

....

....

....

....

....

....

....

....

....

....

....

....

....

....

My favorite book was .... by ....

....

The cover looked like this:

It was about..

....

....

....

....

....

Extracurricular activities I did in my childhood include [soccer, basketball, baseball, teeball, softball, lacrosse, football, gymnastics, ballet, tap, jazz, modern dance, art, music, swimming, acting, Other]..

....

....

....

....

The activity I did the longest was ....

I [enjoyed/did not enjoy] it, because..

....

....

....

....

What I miss most about my favorite childhood hobby, ...

........................., is..

....

....

....

As a kid, I imagined what it would be like to become a(n) ....

....

....

....

My version of that life looked like this: ....

....

....

....

....

....

....

....

....

....

The reason(s) I gave up my favorite hobby/hobbies was/ were: (Circle all that apply) [changing responsibilities, discouragement from continuing, no time, low chances of earning money, low odds of success, too much competition in the hobby's related field, loss of interest, I'm not really sure]..........

....

Old hobbies that I think I'd still enjoy as an adult, even if they have to be modified, include..

....

....

....

....

Some easy ways I can rediscover my old hobbies and inter-

ests might be...

....

....

....

....

....

....

A goal of mine from my childhood or teenage years that I'd

still like to accomplish is..

....

....

....

....

....

....

CHERISHED ITEMS

This subsection might seem less meaningful than the Hobbies one, but it can have the same beneficial effects—just on a smaller scale (the magic of nostalgia at work again!).

A cherished article of clothing/accessory I always wore as a

kid was ....,

....

....

....

....

....

and it had these details...

....

....

....

....

....

My favorite toy or "security item" was ....

....

I'd take it to ....

....

....

....

My favorite things about it were its [scent, sentimentality, softness, the person who gave it to me, how comforted it made me feel, ...]

....

I [still have it/no longer have it]...
My favorite cup/plate to use in our kitchen was ....

....

I remember these details about its appearance...........................

....

....

....

My first or favorite bike was ...., and I got it when .... I [rode it often/didn't use it much], and remember this detail of it more than anything else: ....

....

....

....

....

....

....

....

When I was a kid, I thought the coolest/best thing I owned

was ....

....

....

....

....

....

....

....

because..

....

....

....

....

....

....

....

....

....

HOLIDAY TRADITIONS

The warm, fuzzy feelings of the holidays aren't just something cooked up by big corporations to sell more stuff: research shows the rituals we partake in during those special times actually decrease our anxiety[13] by instilling a sense of predictability.

What's more, because these rituals are done with loved ones, they help us feel more connected and give us a sense of belonging from a young age.[14]

Recalling holiday memories is easy for most of us, because—as mentioned earlier—strong sensory ties serve as signals to our brains to take notes. And holidays and special events are practically guarantees of spectacular sights, sounds, smells, and tastes.

Without a doubt, you can still remember the mouth-watering pies laid out at Thanksgiving, or the scent of candles during Advent, or the crescent moon and contemplative calm of Ramadan. No matter what your family celebrated, those unchanging traditions—many of which you may continue now, with your own family—brought a sense of peace and comfort that still resonates.

---

13 https://www.sciencedirect.com/science/article/abs/pii/
S074959781630437X?via%3Dihub
14 https://www.sciencedirect.com/science/article/abs/pii/
S109051381500077X?via%3Dihub

Before you start this section, take a moment to transport yourself back to those times. Carefully consider each sense, and the memories attached to it: the scent and taste of your favorite holiday meals, the sounds of music and chit-chat from family, the sights of twinkling lights or fresh snow, or even the sensations of touching some treasured holiday items, like favorite ornaments or decor.

The holiday my family always went all out for was ....

....

....

Our traditions for this holiday included ....

....

....

....

....

....

Our Thanksgiving Day usually went like this: ....

....

....

....

....

....

....

....

....

....

....

....

....

....

Our New Year's celebrations were often..

....

....

....

....

....

....

....

....

....

....

....

....

....

....

Lesser holidays we celebrated include ....,

and those entailed...

....

....

....

....

My favorite things about the holidays as a kid were: (Circle all that apply) [Spending time with family, distant relatives visiting, the hustle and bustle in our house, shopping, wrapping gifts, singing songs, revisiting traditions and stories from my family's heritage, the meals we ate, cooking those meals with my family, visiting Santa, opening presents, attending religious services, volunteer work/acts of charity, the excitement and anticipation, parades or special television programs, playing in the snow, getting out of school, ...

....

....

Some decorations I still remember are ....

....

....

....

....

....

The best holiday present I ever got was ....,

from ....

I received it for ....

....

A special holiday memory I revisit often is...................................

....

....

....

....

A funny holiday story I still laugh about to this day is................

....

....

....

....

....

....

....

My favorite holiday movies as a kid included: ....

....

....

To me, the best food we served during the holidays was ....

....

....

....

This is the recipe, or general idea of how it was made: ....

....

....

....

....

If I had to name the most prominent scents of my home during the holidays, they would be: [examples, pine trees, candles, potpourri, family members' colognes and perfumes, turkey, cookies, etc.]..

....

....

A tradition I miss most from my childhood is ....,

....

....

....

....

....

because ....

....

....

....

....

....

....

A childhood tradition I still continue/plan on doing with my

own family is ....

....

....

....

....

....

....

....

....

....

....

....

ELEMENTARY AND MIDDLE OR JUNIOR HIGH SCHOOL

Some of us despised school; some of us loved it. But, for better or for worse, the memories of our early education stick with us more strongly than most others. It's not surprising, since research shows our school years, particularly middle school or junior high, is one of the most formative periods in our lives.[15]

It might be hard to recall memories of school at first, especially if you didn't enjoy it. As with previous sections, it can be helpful to start with the basic facts and go from there. If all you can remember, at first, is the school's name or a particular teacher, that's okay: the rest may fall into place while you write.

---

15 http://www.ascd.org/ASCD/pdf/journals/ed_lead/el_197704_fen-wick.pdf

You might find the opposite holds true—that exact details escape you, while vague sensory information readily jumps to the front of your mind, such as the scent of school bus exhaust, or a colorful mural painted in the library, or the feeling of pure joy when recess finally rolled around.

Start with what you can remember best and go from there. It might be helpful to look up a picture of your old school buildings, if they still exist, or to look through old work or report cards.

The name of my elementary school was ....,

located in ....

....

What it looked like, in my memory, was ....

....

....

....

....

....

I [rode the bus/walked/got dropped off] most days, and I re-member this most vividly about my trips to and from school:

....

....

....

....

....

....

My favorite elementary school teacher was ....

....

....

Something about him/her I still remember or appreciate is....

....

....

....

....

....

....

....

....

My favorite subject in elementary school was [math, reading, writing, science, social studies or history, art, music, gym, computers, typing, other] ....

My best friends from elementary school were ....

....

....

....

....

I met them in..

....

....

....

....

....

....

....

....

On the playground during recess, you'd usually find me............

....

....

My most embarrassing moment in elementary school was,

....

....

....

while my proudest moment was ....

....

....

....

....

People I met in elementary school who I still know today incl

ude...

....

....

....

....

....

....

....

....

The name of my middle school/junior high school was ....,

....

and it was located ....

....

The exterior of the building looked like ....

....

....

....

....

My favorite teacher in middle school was ....,

who taught me .... in the ....

grade. Something about them I still remember/appreciate is.

....

....

....

....

....

....

....

....

....

My favorite subject in middle school was ....,

because..

....

....

....

My best friends from middle school were ....

....

....

....

....

....

....

....

....

I met them when..

....

....

....

....

....

....

....

During lunch or after school, you'd usually find me.....................

....

....

My most embarrassing moment in middle school was when,

....

....

....

....

....

....

and my proudest moment was ....

....

....

....

....

....

People I met in middle school who I still know today include...

....

....

....

....

....

....

My appearance during this time can be described as...................

....

....

....

....

....

....

....

Overall, my experience in middle school or junior high could be summed up in these three words: ....

....

....

My middle school/junior high years helped shape me into who I am today in the following ways: ....

....

....

....

....

....

....

....

....

....

....

....

....

....

CHILDHOOD MISCELLANEA

As we near the end of Part I, you're probably feeling pretty nostalgic for the good ol' years, and definitely *not* looking forward to documenting those awkward teenage ones—so before we bid your childhood adieu, let's dig into a few more odds and ends.

My worst childhood injury was ....,

....

....

....

....

....

....

which I sustained when ....

....

....

....

My [recovery/doctor visit/hospital visit] happened like this
(Include recovery timelines, number of stitches, if you need-
ed a cast, etc.) ....

....

....

....

....

....

....

Some childhood crushes of mine were ....

....

....

....

....

....

....

....

....

....

....

What I liked most about them was ....

....

....

....

....

....

....

....

....

....

....

....

....

I [told them/did not tell them] I liked them. The silliest thing I ever did to get a crush's attention was..

....

....

....

....

....

One of my most memorable "childhood sweethearts" was ....

....

....

....

....

....

who I met when ....

....

....

....

....

....

....

What I remember most about them is...

....

....

....

....

....

....

....

....

....

....

....

....

....

....

If I could tell my childhood self one thing, it would be this: ......

....

....

....

....

....

....

....

....

....

....

....

....

....

....

PART II:
YOUR TEENAGE
YEARS

A h, the teen years: everyone's favorite time.

...said no one, ever.

This section won't be pretty, but it will be insightful. Research shows high school sticks with us in all its awkward, bittersweet glory for many reasons,[16] one of which is how strongly we felt emotions back then. Like children, teenagers tend to feel happiness, sadness, fear, or excitement without restraint. But, unlike children, teens can and do feel several emotions at once, which is why our memories of those years are such a mixed blessing.

Every regret, heartache, and failure is probably still very fresh in your mind—but so are the good times, like how our friends meant more to us than just about anyone else, or how exciting it was to think about our futures and see infinite possibilities.

While it might be tough, try not to linger on the worst of those years: there were undoubtedly great times mixed in, and some experiences and people you miss dearly. As you recall memories for this section, try looking through old yearbooks, digging out Prom photos, or—better yet—listening to the music you loved back then.

Yep: there's a reason all the music of today doesn't sound as good to you as the music you loved in your prime, and it's not because the music's gotten worse. Well...most of it, anyway. Rather, it's largely due to how much neurological growth you experienced as a teen, which imprinted those songs in your memory.[17]

16 *https://theconversation.com/why-high-school-stays-with-us-forever-56538*
17 *https://slate.com/technology/2014/08/musical-nostalgia-the-psychology-and-neuroscience-for-song-preference-and-the-reminiscence-bump.html*

Not only does it release dopamine and other feel-good neurochemicals, but it also boosts brain function (your neurons actually sync to the beat of songs you enjoy)[18], which will make memory recall easier.

So dig out your old records, CDs, or iPod, crank a playlist, and dive into what might turn out to be your favorite section of this entire journal.

18 https://www.scientificamerican.com/podcast/episode/brain-rhythms-sync-to-musical-beat/

I went to high school at ....,

located ....

Our school colors were ....,

and our mascot was ....

....

As a teen, I was:

[Unpopular, popular, somewhere in between]

[Cool, nerdy, some of each]

[Studious, a slacker]

[A rule follower, a troublemaker]

[Attentive to trends, marching to my own beat]

[A social butterfly, very shy, a mix of both]

[Desperate to fit in, uncaring about social status, somewhere

in the middle]

[Quiet, loud]

[Adventurous, reserved]

....

....

....

....

....

My friends during this time were ....

....

....

....

....

....

....

....

I'm still in touch with these friends from high school: ....

....

....

....

....

....

....

....

Some of the best times I ever had with my friends were.............

....

....

....

....

....

....

....

....

....

The activities I enjoyed in high school were: (Circle all that apply) [Lacrosse, football, baseball, softball, soccer, basketball, tennis, choir, track and field, drama club, yearbook/newspaper/student publications, drill team, cheerleading, step, flag girls/majorettes, marching band, orchestra, foreign language, student government, art club, tech programs, leadership programs, creative writing, chemistry/science club, home economics, Other ....

....

....]

My fondest memories of high school took place in ....

....

....

with my friends ....

....

....

....

....

....

....

....

....

What I miss most about this is...

....

....

....

....

....

....

....

....

....

....

My favorite teacher in high school was ...., who

taught me .... in the ....

grade. What I loved most about him/her was..............................

....

....

....

....

....

After school, you'd almost always find me......................................

....

....

....

....

....

My favorite after-school food was ....

....

....

....

....

....

....

One trait that made me stand out from my peers was ....

....

....

....

Jobs I held during high school or the summers included............

....

....

....

....

An experience from my teen years I still cringe about is.............

....

....

....

....

....

....

....

....

Something that upset or embarrassed me a lot back then, but that I now realize wasn't that bad, is ....

....

....

....

....

....

....

What I miss most about high school is ....,

....

....

....

....

but I don't miss ....

....

....

....

....at all.

My favorite bands or artists as a teenager were ....

....

....

....

....

....

....

....

I still listen to ....

....

....

....

....

....

....

....

on a regular basis.

What I enjoyed about or connected with most in that music was...

....

....

....

....

....

....

....

That music made me feel...

....

....

....

....

....

....

....

....

One song or album I can still listen to and feel like a teenager

again is ....

....

If I had to create a soundtrack for my high school experience,

these tracks would be on it: ....

....

....

....

....

....

....

....

....

....

....

....

....

....

....

....

....

....

....

....

....

....

....

My first concert was [musician] .... with

[people] ....,

....

....

at ....

....

I remember this detail about it the most: ....

....

....

....

....

....

....

....

Movies I went to see in high school include.......................................

....

....

....

....

....

One of the biggest pieces of gossip/scandals I remember floating around my school was...

....

....

....

....

....

....

A rumor or urban legend from my school was...............................

....

....

....

....

....

....

....

....

....

My favorite Prom was [junior/senior]. I went with [people]

....

....

....

....

It was held at [location] ....

....,

and the theme was ....

....

....

....

My outfit that night was ....

....

....

....

....

My biggest teenage crush was on ....

....

I [told/didn't tell] them. Something I still remember liking

about them is..

....

....

....

....

My worst teenage heartbreak was from ....

....,

when I was .... years old. ....

....

helped me get through it by..

....

....

....

....

Learning to drive was [stressful, exciting]. The car I [pur-

chased, was given, borrowed, was allowed to use] was a [col-

or] .... [year, make, and model] ....

....

This detail about the car stands out most to me: ....

....

....

....

....

As a young driver, I was [cautious, overconfident, slow, too

fast, reckless, careful]..

My sense of style in high school was...

....

....

....

....

The biggest ways I changed between freshman and senior

years were..

....

....

....

....

On my graduation day, I remember thinking ....

....

....

....

....

....

A trait I developed as a teen that became a large part of my

adulthood is ....

....

....

....

....

If I could tell my teenage self one thing, it would be......................

....

....

....

....

....

....

....

....

....

PART III: COLLEGE/EARLY ADULTHOOD

Much like our teen years, the time between age 18 and 22 or so is often fraught with mistakes and embarrassments, but also occupies a large piece of our memories. Neuroscience calls this time period the "reminiscence bump"—those years we remember more sharply than most of the years to follow.[19]

Not only did most of our neurological development finish in this timeframe, but we also discovered invaluable truths about ourselves. College and early adulthood are where we learned who we were, what we stood for, and what we were capable of.

If you didn't attend college, feel free to skip or modify those questions. Just because you didn't take a course that challenged your perspective, for example, doesn't mean you never experienced anything similar: think of coworkers or roommates you met during those years, or anyone who made you shift your way of thinking and grow into the person you are today.

The next section will cover your twenties more thoroughly, so try to limit these answers to those crucial 4 years between teen and young adult—even if your time at college went on for longer than that, or not at all.

19 https://slate.com/technology/2013/01/reminiscence-bump-explanations-why-we-remember-young-adulthood-better-than-any-other-age.html

I went to college/trade school at ....

....,

located in ....

....

I chose this school because..

....

....

....

....

....

I lived [at home/in a rented apartment or house/in a dorm]
most of this time. My roommates were ....

....

....

....

....

....

....

What I loved most about where I lived was..................................

....
..

....

....

....

....

....

In school, I studied ....

....

....

....

....

.... I

chose this field of study because ....

....

....

....

....

....

....

....

....

A class I took there challenged my perspective on ....

....

by ....

....

....

....

It was during this time period that I learned this really important truth about myself: ....

....

....

....

....

....

....

....

One of my best accomplishments from these years is ....

....

....

....

....

One of my biggest mistakes was ....

....

....

....

....,

but I learned this valuable lesson out of it: ....

....

....

....

....

A course or field of study that interested me, despite not being my chosen field, was ....

....

....

I didn't explore it further because ....

....

....

....

....

A huge factor in my transition to independence was ....

....

....

During finals week or times of stress, you'd usually find me....

....

....

Some interesting facts or skills I learned in school that I still

use today are...

....

....

....

....

....

....

....

....

....

My style during this time was..

....

....

....

One way I was too hard on myself back then is ....

....

....

....

Adults I really looked up during this time include ....

....

....

....

....

....

....

....

....

When I compared my life to that of my peers and friends, I
thought I was doing [better/worse/the same] because ....

....

....

Something brand-new I experienced during this time, even
if it later became mundane, was ....

....

....

....

....

....

....

....

....

I think this stuck with me because ....

....

....

....

....

....

....

Somewhere unique or fun I travelled was ....

....

....

....

....

....

....

What I loved about it most was ....

....

....

....

....

....

....

....

....

....

....

If I could tell my 18- to 22-year-old self one thing, it would be

....

....

....

....

....

....

....

PART IV:
TWENTIES
AND THIRTIES

Most of our childhoods and early adulthoods look similar: we can all recall playing with siblings or cousins, snuggling up with beloved pets, the drudgery of early morning bus rides, or the sights and scents of favorite holidays. We all had awkward stages, crushes, and heartbreaks; most of us learned to drive at the same time, and attended Proms and graduations.

But this is where everyone's autobiographical memories start to diverge: the late twenties and early thirties.

From age 23 to about 35, some people had children or got married; some opted to focus on their careers. Some took that time to travel, work various jobs, or discover more about themselves.

One thing's for certain, though: virtually none of us knew what we were doing, at least not until our third decade of life (and many would argue you never *quite* figure it out completely).

In this section, you'll notice memories don't come as easily as they did in the first parts of this journal. This is that reminiscence bump at work again: by our late twenties, we usually settle into some kind of routine, and have experienced enough things for events to stop feeling so novel. This means your brain "took fewer notes" as time went on.

Granted, this won't hold true for everyone—and it's impossible to say when, exactly, our memories stop being so vivid and frequent. For that reason, some of these entries will be broader than previous sections. Feel free to drill down into specifics wherever they pop up, or keep your answers vague if need be.

Lastly, if some questions don't apply to these years (say, if you met your spouse in your forties), fill it out anyway, and make a note of your actual age at the time. You can also skip questions like those, if they're not applicable.

After college/trade school/entering the workforce, I spent some time..

....

....

....

....

My goals during this time were mainly ....

....

....

....

....

....

Something about living on my own that I didn't expect was.......

....

....

....

Something I think I did very well while exploring my new independence was ....

....

....

....

One new adult responsibility I was afraid of or disliked was

....,

because ....

....

....

....

In my mid-twenties, I was: (Circle all that apply) [fun-loving, free-spirited, focused on work, into casual dating, looking to settle down, traveling, driven, aimless, confident, insecure, reckless, responsible, into partying or nightlife, into more low-key activities, a night owl, an early riser, in-the-moment, focused on the future] ....

The moment I realized I wasn't a kid anymore was when ....

....

....

During this time, I noticed this new or emerging trait about myself that came from my [mother/father]: ....

....

....

....

....

....

....

My most-frequented club, bar, or restaurant in my twenties

was ....

....

....

....

....,

located in ....

....

....

....

While there, I'd usually ....

....

....

....

....

....

....

....

....

My social group in my late twenties and early thirties con-
sisted of ....

....

....

I remember thinking this when I turned 30: ....
Something I accomplished during these years I'm very proud
of is ....

....

....

....

....

....

....

....

I met my spouse at the age of ....,
when ....

....

....

....

....

....

When we started dating, I [knew right away we'd be great to-gether/needed some convincing]...

What first attracted me to them was ....

....

....

....

....

I think what first attracted them to me was my ....

....

....

....

I proposed/they proposed to me at [location] ....

.... by ....

We got married on [date] ....

Our wedding was [big, small], and held at [location] ....

....

I can remember these details about our engagement, the wedding party, the ceremony, and/or reception: ....

....

....

....

....

....

....

Our best or favorite wedding gift was ....

....

....

Our first home together can best be described as: (Circle all that apply) [Cozy, cramped, spacious, dilapidated, charming, regrettable, safe, unsafe, clean, messy, private, crowded, well-furnished, bare bones, stylish, basic, cheap, expensive] During our first year as a married couple, we argued frequently about ....

....

Something we always agreed upon was ....

....

....

....

Our first child was born on ....

I remember feeling ....

....

....

when we discovered we were expecting..

In the delivery room, I was [calm/nervous]. The birth of our

first child went like this...

....

....

....

I remember holding our child and thinking ....

....

....

....

As a new parent, I was [confident/unsure] in my abilities be-

cause ....

....

....

....

....

When our first child learned to ....

....,

I felt ....

....

....

....

My spouse and I had these strengths as young parents:

me	my spouse	both

The funniest story from my time as a new parent is ....

....

....

....

....

....

....

....

The birth experiences of my other children entailed ....

....

....

....

....

....

....

Through the years, my spouse and I learned ....

....

....

....

....

....

....

....

....

....

Our first purchased home was located in ....

....

This is what it looked like ....

....

....

....

....

....

....

....

My career during this time was ....

....

....

....

I enjoyed it most because of its ....

....

....

....

....,

but disliked its ....

....

....

....

One way I really came into my own during this time period is

....

....

By my early thirties, my life [was/wasn't] what I expected or

planned it to be, because ....

....

....

....

....

....

One thing I wish I'd done more of in my late twenties or early

thirties is ....

....

....

Overall, I think my twenties were about ....

....

....,

while my thirties were more about ....

....

....

When my kids are this age, my main advice to them will be to

....

....

....

....

....

....

PART V: FORTIES AND FIFTIES

They say life begins at 40, and in many ways, the adage holds up. You're more confident in who you are as a person, and know what you want from life. Financially, you're probably in far better shape than the last decade, making many of your goals and dreams more achievable.

More than anything, though, you have wisdom. The mistakes and pitfalls of one's twenties and thirties teach valuable lessons (sometimes repeatedly). By age 40, we've learned our worth in the workplace, cut a toxic person or two out of our lives, and stood up for others—spouses or children, for example—enough to now do the same for ourselves.

Additionally, we stop needing validation or approval as much as we used to.[20] We're less afraid to speak our minds, more willing to say "no" when we need to, and less concerned with looking cool or successful, especially if it requires doing things that don't align with our true selves.

Of course, that golden decade isn't without its own trials and tribulations. Most people experience a midlife crisis of sorts around age 47 or so,[21] or a noticeable drop in happiness for a few years into our fifties.

The answer may lie in biology or declining physical fitness. It could be kids moving out, leaving us with an empty nest, or our own parents requiring medical attention. Marriages may end, or health crises might crop up. If our teens and twenties are the years of believing we're invincible, our forties and fifties are the years of realizing we're absolutely *not*.

But, for all the challenges those decades bring, there are plenty of upsides. That confidence and strong sense of self

20 https://www.lifehack.org/297777/8-undeniable-reasons-your-40s-are-your-golden-decade
21 https://greatergood.berkeley.edu/article/item/why_were_unhappiest_in_our_late_40s

can be parlayed into new careers, smart investments, reconnections with spouses or old friends, a newfound health consciousness, and much more.

It's true that life between 40 and 60 feels like the second act in a play...but we all know that's when the story gets really good.

By age 40, I'd learned this about myself: ....

....

....

....

....

....

Something I stopped caring about in my 40s that used to feel

really important was ....

....

....

....

....

....

....

Something I started caring about, that I dismissed before, was

....

....

....

....

....

....

My marriage changed during my 40s in the following ways:......

....

....

....

....

When I turned 40, I remember thinking ....

....

....

....

....

....

....

....

A new hobby or interest I picked up in my 40s or 50s was ...

....

....

....

....

What I enjoyed most about it was ....

....

....

....

....

My career saw these changes during my 40s and 50s: ....

....

....

....

....

....

....

....

....

....

....

....

....

....

One aspect of my life I was suddenly really fired up to change

was: ....

....

....

I stopped being afraid to ....

....

....,

because ....

....

....

....

Some difficult challenges I faced during these years were ....

....

....

....

....

....

....

....

....

....

....

My relationship with my parents [improved/worsened] be-

cause ....

....

....

....

....

....

....

....

As my kids grew/became teenagers, my parenting style be-

came more ....

....,

and less ....

....

I'm proud of how I ....

....

....,

and think I could have improved on ....

....

....

An activity, person, or aspect of my life that helped me feel

really content and fulfilled was ....

....

....

I handled turning 40 [well/not well], because ....

....

....

....

By the time I turned 50, I'd learned this about myself ....

....

....

....

....

My priorities in my 40s and 50s shifted from ....

....

....

to ....

....

....,

mostly due to ....

....

....

....

By age 50, I'd finally grasped this: ....

....

....

....

....

....

....

....

Something I accomplished in my 40s or 50s I never thought

possible   was   ....

....

....

....

....

PART VI: SIXTY AND BEYOND

If you breezed through your 40s and 50s, you might not be worried about entering your seventh decade—or, like most people, you'll feel a strange mixed reaction, both components of which are perfectly valid.

One half of that reaction will be pride: a sense of accomplishment from how far you've come and all the milestones you've passed along the way. On the other hand, you might also notice some regrets, a feeling like time is running out, or a looming sadness that everything seems downhill from here. Part of this is due to the noticeable physical decline that hits most people around age 60, when health problems become more pronounced, and blood protein levels decrease.[22]

(*Psst*, don't worry: pundits say 70 is the new 60, and that, statistically speaking, most won't see nearly as sharp a decline as their own parents or grandparents experienced, particularly if they've been taking care of themselves in decades prior.[23] It's also never too late to start—a 35-year Swedish study[24] found that men who were late-starters to exercise experienced the same benefits after 5 years as those who started prior to age 50.)

Physical changes aside, there's another inevitable shift that might get you feeling down: a drop in cognitive abilities. Memory gets trickier. While your childhood through your 20s or 30s still plays vividly in your head, you'll notice the 40s through present are a little murky.

---

22 https://newatlas.com/science/ageing-blood-protein-changes-age-34-60-78/
23 https://www.scientificamerican.com/article/is-70-really-the-new-60/
24 https://www.health.harvard.edu/mens-health/never-too-late-exercise-helps-late-starters

This doesn't mean there was nothing worth remembering, however (just your brain lingering on that reminiscence bump again). You've experienced just as many incredible things past age 40, and past 60, as you did in your youth: career fulfillment, retirement, anniversaries, and watching your own kids become parents are more treasured than every wild party or carefree vacation you took back in the day, even if the details aren't as sharp.

This section will feel like the broadest of all, but with good reason. You now have unique abilities you didn't before: wisdom, hindsight, and an unshakeable sense of self even 50-year-old you couldn't match. You're capable of looking back on your life with unbeatable clarity—not in the little details, necessarily, but in the way that matters most: how those times made you feel.

When I turned 60, I knew this about myself, without a doubt:..

....

....

....

....

....

....

....

Turning 60 was [challenging/not challenging] because ....

....

....

....

My favorite age, if I had to choose, was .... This

is why: ....

....

....

....

....

....

....

....

....

....

....

My life changed radically in my 60s because of these events: (Example: birth of grandchildren, loss of parents, health changes, etc.) ....

....

....

....

....

....

....

....

I most enjoy these hobbies in my older age: ....

....

....

....

....

....

....

....

....

Something that frightens me about aging is ....

....

....

....

....

....

....,

but something I look forward to/enjoy immensely is ....

....

....

....

....

....

....,

because ....

....

....

....

....

....

....

....

....

My marriage is ....

....

....

....

....

....

....

....

When I look back on our journey from newlyweds to now, I think something we did very well was ....

....

....

....

....

....

....

....

If I had to give my own children or future generations one piece of advice to make marriage work, either because of my own marriage's successes or failures, it would be this: ....

....

....

....

....

....

....

As of [date of writing] ...., I have .... grandchildren: ....

....

....

....

....

....

....

....

Becoming a grandparent felt ....

....

....

....

....

Something I do much differently as a grandparent than I did

as a parent is ....

....

....

....

....

....

....

....

....

Watching my children become parents, I think they've done

this exceptionally well: ....

....

....

....

....

....

....

I wish, based on my own experiences as a parent, they would

consider my advice more in regards to ....

....

....

....

....

....

....

....

....

because ....

....

....

....

....

....

....

....

My retirement looks/will look like ....

....

....

....

....

....

....

....

In retrospect, my career path seems ....

....

....

....

....

....

....

If I could change one thing about my career, it would be ....

....

....

....

Financially, I made some very smart moves such as ....

....

....

....

....

....

....

....,

but a few mistakes, too, like ....

....

....

....

....

....

....

....

One piece of financial advice I want to leave my kids and grandkids is this: ....

....

....

....

....

....

....

When my grandchildren enter young adulthood, I want them

to know that ....

....

....

....

....

....

....

In my 60s, 70s, or 80s, I realized this about my parents that

didn't occur to me before: ....

....

....

....

....

....

....

If I could tell my mother one thing, it would be ....

....

If I could tell my father one thing, it would be ....

....

My biggest regret is ....

....

....

....

....,

because ....

....

....

....

....

....

One positive effect I can name from this, however, is that .....

....

....

....

....

....

What I most want to be remembered for is ....

....

....

....

....

....

....

....

....

....

....

....

As I read through my previous entries in this journal, I think/
feel that ....

....

....

....

....

....

....

....

....

....

....

....

....

....

....

....

....

....

....

When my loved ones read this, I hope they walk away with

the impression that ....

....

....

....

....

....

....

Being as objective as possible, I look back on each period in

my life and can sum it up thusly: ....

Decade/Age	Summary

PART VII:
EXTRAS

This section is a bit of a catch-all, but nonetheless important. In it, you'll explore your heritage, future goals, and more—and find places to leave notes for the loved ones who will inherit your journal.

As stated in the introductory sections, you can fill these pages out at any time, or split it up across multiple decades. You can also choose to add to each entry over time: for example, you may choose to fill out your Bucket List with a few items at ages 20, 30, 40, and onward. This approach can be fun and extremely insightful, as it provides a compilation of all the "yous" through the years.

CULTURE AND HERITAGE

Our culture is an important piece of who we are, whether or not we feel a deep connection with those roots. Indeed, even if we don't *know* our roots, we've all had moments where certain traditions or cultures spoke to us, in a way that almost felt spiritual. There's a shared history with other members of our culture, and a gravity in knowing we're an important link in an ongoing chain.

Neuroscience is on your side with this one, too: connecting with our culture instills a greater sense of belonging, and has the same benefits as general nostalgia on cognitive function.[25] Preliminary research suggests the sense of authenticity we feel by connecting to our roots makes us happier, perhaps because it provides concrete evidence of who we are and how we came to be.

If you don't know your heritage, it's okay to keep it broad or guess, based on whatever information you do have. For instance, tracing your surname's origins or researching certain traditions might give you enough clues to make an educated guess on where your family came from.

25   https://www.sciencedirect.com/topics/social-sciences/cultural-heritage

Where my family immigrated from, and in which generation (mine, my parents', grandparents', great-grandparents', etc.):

Mother's Side: ....

....

....

....

....

....

....

Father's Side: ....

....

....

....

....

....

To the best of my knowledge, my family immigrated because

....

....

....

....

....

....

....

....

....

....

....

I first became aware of our heritage around age ....

My first memory of this is ....

....

....

....

....

My heritage impacted my childhood [a lot/some/not much]

because ....

....

....

....

....

....

....

....

....

....

....

My culture and family's origins impact me today in these
ways: ....

....

....

....

....

....

....

More than anything, I want my kids, grandkids, and future
generations to remember this about our roots ....

....

....

....

....

....

POLITICALS VIEWS AND DEEPEST VALUES/BELIEFS

This can be a polarizing sub-section, to say the least! For every person out there who loves discussing politics, there's one or two (or several) who absolutely detest it.

No matter which camp you fall into, don't breeze through these questions under the assumption you're 100% certain of your answers: you might surprise yourself. And don't power through just because you just want to get this part over with as fast as possible.

Consider your answers carefully. This isn't just to state *what* you believe, but *why*—a place to encapsulate all the nuances, exceptions, and even doubts that a heated Thanksgiving argument doesn't allow.

You'll also find entries that touch on your beliefs in a broader sense, and even a few ethical conundrums, that won't just help future generations understand why you believed what you did; it might help you understand it better, too.

In a word, I'd describe my political stance as ....

....

....

I believe our country would benefit most from these three

things: ....

....

....

....

These are the leaders that have been in power during my

lifetime: ....

....

....

....

....

....

....

....

In my opinion, the best leader I've seen in action so far was

....,

while the worst was ....

....

A leader I didn't agree with politically, but liked as a person, was ....

....

A leader I had high hopes for who disappointed me was ....

....,

due to ....

....

....

....

My political views have changed over time in these ways: ......

....

....

Overall, I think these 3 personality traits of mine are why I believe what I do: ....

....

....

....

When it comes to right and wrong, I think most situations [are very black and white, with no room to argue; fall into a gray area, where context matters a lot]. ....

....

....

I abide laws [regardless of whether or not I agree with them; that make sense, but ignore a few that don't]. This is because

....

....

I'm [okay/not okay] with small white lies where no one gets hurt, because ....

....

....

I think today's society is ....

....

....

....

I value these 7 things most: (Circle 7) [honesty, integrity, work ethic, personal responsibility, charity, kindness, faith, optimism, realism, facts and reason, feelings and intuition, law and order, free will, the environment, animal rights, human rights, family and friends, career, Other: ....

....]

Many people assume I believe ....

....,

but what I actually believe/some context they don't understand is ....

....

....

....

....

What makes a good person is ....

....

....

....

Overall, I think I'm a [good/bad/neutral] person, because ...

....

....

....

....

....

....

....

....

One area in which I doubt my beliefs is ....

....

....

....

PEOPLE

There are over 7 billion people on this planet, and the average person will encounter 80,000 of them in their lifetime.[26]

Of course, most of them won't be memorable: that guy you made small talk with in the elevator, or the receptionist who walked you through some insurance forms, aren't exactly critical or life-changing interactions. But some were. And of those 80,000, you forged deep, meaningful connections with at least a handful of people, and influenced many of them in turn.

In this section, you'll encounter prompts to recall some of those connections, and write about the souls who helped enrich your time on this big blue marble.

---

26 https://blog.adioma.com/counting-the-people-you-impact-info-graphic/#:~:text=Is%20it%20a%20lot%3F,have%20what%20you%20can%20offer.

The people I've lost during my life who I miss most include ....

....

....

....

....

....

....

....

....

....

The most selfless act I've ever witnessed was ....

....

....

The kindest or most thoughtful thing another person ever did for me was ....

....

....

What gives me faith in humanity and hope for the future is ....

....

....

....

....

....

....

....

....

The top 5 greatest influences in my life were ....

....

....

....

....,

and this is how they each shaped who I became ....

....

....

....

....

....

....

....

....

....

Celebrities or historical figures I've always admired include

....

....

....

....

....

....

....

The most successful person I know in real life is ....,

due to their ....

....

....

If I was only guaranteed one more day, I'd spend it with ....

....

....

....

Someone who inspired me to become a better person is ....

....

....

....

....,

because ....

....

....

....

....

....

....

....

One person I wish I'd spent more time or reconciled with is

....

....

If I could, I'd tell them ....

....

....

....

An interaction with a total stranger that I still remember to

this day is ....

....

....

....

....

....

....

The people who have always been there for me, without fail,

are ....

....

....

....

....

....

....

....

....

....

....

....

....

....

....

MY BUCKET LIST

In this subsection, you'll write down all the goals and dreams you hope to accomplish during your life. It's okay if you aren't sure about a few, or if they change later.

If you're filling this part out at an age where you feel you've accomplished most/all of your goals, you can choose to write out those goals retroactively—or list a few things you still hope to do. It's never too late!

Finally, don't feel limited to only listing items directly in your control. If one of your dreams is to become a grandparent, for example, you can absolutely write that down. Likewise, no dream is too small. Learning to cook is just as valid as traveling the world.

A few items are suggested to stoke those creative fires, but you'll notice most of the lines are blank. If you get stuck, think about each of your accomplishments so far: what would make them even better?

I want to learn to do this new activity: ....

....

....

....

....

....

....

I want to change this about myself: ....

....

....

....

....

....

....

I want to revisit this hobby/passion: ....

....

....

....

....

....

....

....

....

I want to travel to this place: ....

....

....

....

....

....

....

....

....

....

....

....

....

....

....

....

....

My Bucket List

SOME THOUGHTS AND NOTES TO MY SPOUSE

I really love this about you: ....

....

....

....

....

....

....

....

....

Something I've always wondered about you or our marriage,

but never asked you, is ....

....

....

....

....

....

....

....

....

My greatest fear during our marriage is/was ....

....

....

....

....

....

You are the [adjective - strongest, smartest, sweetest, most

loyal, etc.] ....

.... person I know.

To this day, I can't fathom how you ....

....

....

....

You've enriched my life by ....

....

....

....

I regret this in our relationship: ....

....

....

....

....

A storm we weathered together was ....

....

....

I admired the way you ....

....

....

When I see your smile, I ....

....

....

When I go, I want you to remember this more than anything

else: ....

....

....

....

....

....

A NOTE TO MY KIDS

Here is where you can speak directly to your children, the people most likely to receive this journal after your passing.

While completing this section, avoid legalities; it's tempting to focus on black-and-white facts like inheritance or final wishes, but that's not what this journal is about (although, if you'd like a place to include information like that, this After Death Planner [https://www.amazon.com/dp/1081837160] is ideal).

Instead, focus on the emotions you want to leave with your kids when they read this. Express pride in their accomplishments, predict the kind of adults they will be, or simply reassure them of your love.

....

....

....

....

....

....

....

FOR MY GRANDKIDS

Dear

....

....

....

....

....

....

....

....

....,

When you read my autobiographical journal, I hope that you

are left with this impression of me: ....

Above all else, I want you to know that ....

....

....

....

....

....

....

....

Never take this for granted: ....

....

....

....

....

....

....

As you progress through your own life, my best advice is to ....

....

....

....

....

....

....

You bring immense joy to my life in the following ways: ....

....

....

....

....

....

....

....

....

....

....

Based on my relationship with my own parents, and the experience and wisdom I gleaned from becoming a parent myself, I want you to remember this about your parents ....

....

....

....

....

....

....

....

....

....

....

....

....

TO FUTURE GENERATIONS

My greatest hopes for our family's legacy are ....

....

....

....

....

....

My wish for our family in another 50 years is: ....

....

....

....

....

....

....

....

....

In another 100 years, I hope the world has improved in the

following ways: ....

....

....

....

....

....

....

....

....

....

....

....

To my great-grandchildren and every generation to follow: I hope you know this about where you come from ....

....

....

....

....

....

....

....

....

FINAL THOUGHTS

As you complete your autobiographical journal, you might stumble across memories that either have no "proper" spot, or that you filled out differently before, but have a new perspective on now.

Or, perhaps, you have more to say to your kids and future generations than previous sections allowed. You can also leave detailed instructions on what's to be done with this journal after you pass.

Maybe you'd just like to share a funny story or two—and that's perfectly fine. There's no wrong purpose for these pages.

....

....

....

....

....

....

....

....

....

....

....

....

....

....

....

....

....

....

....

....

CONCLUSION

CONCLUSION

Making it this far requires some serious congratulations: you slogged through those awkward teen years, dredged up some regrets and painful recollections, and demonstrated a raw honesty not many people have the fortitude to find. It's tough to hold up that magnifying glass on ourselves, and even tougher to do it without some rose-colored spectacles.

What you've just completed, difficult as the journey was, is a wholly unique and accurate version of your own life, totally through your eyes. There is no other story on this earth like the one in your hands, right at this moment.

But...now what?

Who reads your autobiographical journal, and when, is entirely up to you. You might choose to place it with your will and other final documents, only allowing it to see the light of day after you're gone (sparing yourself any embarrassment when your loved ones read about all those cringe-worthy crushes). Or, instead, you might like a few select people to read it now: your spouse, your oldest child, or a grandchild with whom you'd like to form a stronger connection.

It's also acceptable to never show this journal to anyone, if you wish; it can simply be a record of your life and memories for you to enjoy, and you alone.

But what then, you may ask, was the point of filling it out at all?

As stated earlier, reading in general—whether it's a beloved thriller or inspiring non-fiction account, or a journal we've written ourselves—improves memory, cognition, and happiness by strengthening our synapses, creating new ones, and broadening our horizons.[27]

Even better: journaling helps us reveal our truest selves,[28] and that authenticity increases happiness, as well.

That's not to say you haven't been your "true self" prior to encountering this book—just that, perhaps, you didn't yet fully know who that person was. After completing this journal, you do.

And that alone is worth every last pen stroke, on every last page.

27 https://jrelibrary.com/articles/benefits-of-read-ing-why-you-should-read-more/#:~:text=Reading%20improves%20 your%20memory.names%2C%20relationships%2C%20and%20plots.
28 https://whyy.org/segments/can-diaries-reveal-our-true-selves/

Made in United States
Troutdale, OR
03/19/2024

18590637R00139